GONE IN A. . . . .

SO WHAT HAPPENS NEXT?

A true story revealing a bridge of love between two worlds.

By

ANGELA WIGNALL

New Generation Publishing

For Jessica

Who continues to shine!

CONTENTS

INTRODUCTION

During October 2010, at the beginning of her final year studying at university, my beautiful, bright and bubbly daughter Jessica died, almost instantly, in a tragic accident, the day before her twenty second birthday.

Somehow, I found the strength to help my family, at this most devastating time in all our lives. That strength came from my knowledge that Jessica had gone on into the next stage of her 'life' and that I would see her again one day.

Writing funny and entertaining poems for my family and friends has given me great pleasure over the years. I found that when Jessica died, I was able to express my grief through poetry. Not only was this therapeutic, but it enabled me to create something special. The message that my lovely daughter still thrives, somewhere out there, in our wonderful, mystical universe!

I would like to share with you some of my poems and the true story of how Jessica has given us the gift of knowing she 'survives'. I hope anyone who has lost a loved one will find not only enjoyment, but comfort and hope within these pages.

BUILDING THE BRIDGE

I have always been interested in what happens to us when we die from a very young age, reading many books concerning cosmology, the afterlife and constantly asking questions. So I was more than ready thirty years ago, when I had a wonderful spiritual experience, which gave me the knowledge that 'life' goes on after the 'death' of the physical body.

Also at this time, I was introduced to a truly lovely lady who happened to be a medium. A medium is someone who can receive messages from our deceased loved ones and pass them on to us, a bit like a telephone!

I continued to visit my friend the medium, perhaps every couple of years, particularly when I was feeling low. She would relay uplifting messages of comfort and love from relatives or relatives of friends, who had passed on. I always left her home with a feeling of wonder and peace.

Over the years, my husband and I were blessed with two healthy children, a boy and a girl.

Jessica and I were very close in our mother and daughter relationship and clearly loved each other very much, but we argued all the time! During her teenage years, we only had to be in the same room for two minutes and sparks would fly!

It was a challenge for both of us to strive for harmony in the home, but I believed that in the future, perhaps when she had a family of her own, things would calm down.

As Jessica's departure for university drew near, I felt compelled to write this first poem which follows her life from birth to when she left home in September 2008. The original poem had a funny ending, but I re-wrote the last verse especially, as the poem was read to the congregation at Jessica's funeral. It is important to take note that I make reference to her as a STAR.

Time Moves On

Time moves on
and she's going away.
How will I not see her
everyday.

She's a babe in my arms,
all cuddly and soft.
She has a big smile
and she laughs quite a lot!

As a toddler
so stubborn,
won't do what I say.
A nightmare to dress her,
pull my hair out all day!

As she grows she is clever,
a good girl at school.
She gives them no trouble,
a STAR as a rule.

The teens have been turmoil,
so many exams.
But she's worked very hard,
lots of A's she has crammed.

A year off she wanted,
to travel and rest.
To experience the real world
and she's done her best!

Now she is leaving,
an adventure before her.
The nest is too small
for mother and daughter!

But, every day,
I will think of my beautiful girl,
wish her love, wish her joy,
and I know she'll do well.

Composed by Angela September 2008

SIGNS OF 'LIFE'

On the night Jessica died, it was the police who had the burden of bringing us the news of the tragic accident.

I remember my first thought was of how shocked she would be. One minute enjoying lively conversation and laughter with all her young friends, with her future before her. Then, suddenly, to be transported into another dimension, possibly greeted by my mum, who had passed on a few years before!

I asked Jessica to send us a sign that she was safe.

Later that night, the next day and over the coming weeks, our family had many physical signs that Jessica was still around us! The sign that I would like to share with you, is the sign of the STAR.

A few days after her passing, my husband and I were sharing a cup of tea with Jessica's two young flatmates. We had gone to Jessica's house to bring home her belongings. In the little living room they all shared, I noticed a white board on the wall with the girls three names written on it, beside Jessica's name was drawn a large star.

The next day my husband returned from a bike ride and said "I don't know where these socks came from, but they're not mine". The socks he had put on that morning were black with a large silver shining star on the ankle. They were Jessica's, but in all the twenty two years of us living together as a family, Jessica's socks had never been in my husband's sock drawer.

Shortly after that incident, I was hoovering in our breakfast room and I moved the table. Underneath on the carpet was a large golden star!

The most amazing star was found on our first visit to Jessica's memorial plaque. In the little church yard, just under her name, we placed a pink rose. As we were about to leave, for some reason, I bent and picked up a flower pot next to ours to remove some old leaves, and underneath was a shiny gold star! How could there be a star in a church yard in the middle of the forest!

If you allow yourself to be open to receive signs that your loved ones are still around you, they rejoice in making this connection!

The stars have continued to appear over the last few years. At family occasions, at work and when I am very low. I cannot explain how this happens, but we all take huge comfort from the appearance of the stars and of course, I keep them all!

SO WHAT HAPPENS NEXT?

Before I begin, I would like to emphasize that these are only my views, based on my own experiences and many years of research.

I have come to the conclusion that the universe is made up of tiny particles of energy, vibrating at different speeds. When our physical body dies, our soul, or the energy essence of 'us', is released into the next energy level! I am no scientist, but that is the easiest way I can explain what I have learnt. When our loved ones wish to communicate through a medium, they have to lower their speed of vibration.

Books concerning near-death experiences and the afterlife tell us that there are many levels of continuing existence after 'death'.

Like attracts like, therefore, we naturally gravitate to a level where we will be in harmony with all those already 'living' there. How we conduct ourselves here on earth will dictate which level we transfer to. Individuals who have chosen to pursue a life of crime for instance, will go to lower and darker levels. Most of us, however, will enjoy a world similar to this one, but full of amazing and vibrant colours, peace and love.

I have also read many books on different religions and attended a Baptist church for eight years. I have found I am most comfortable with the Spiritualist way of living life here on earth and their views on what happens to us when we die.

When someone attends a Spiritualist church, not only do they receive 'survival' evidence, but words of wisdom and encouragement that we can relate to in our everyday lives. Love is at the centre of everything I have experienced in these churches.

I started to attend a Spiritualist church about ten years ago and it was here that Jessica came to let me know she is 'alive' and 'well' in her new world!

Driving to the church one day, a few weeks after Jessica's 'death', I felt a very strong feeling of love surrounding me. As I sat amongst the congregation, I experienced a divine sense of myself, radiating love!

The medium that day was a young man and I thought if Jessica wanted to come through with a message, it would be from him, as he was handsome as well as being young! After a little while of giving messages to others in the congregation, he came to me. "I have a very bubbly young girl here, she is about twenty two – she says she is so excited that you are here today."

It was my Jessica! Everything he said was true, things that only Jessica and I would have known. Jessica relayed that she was well and vibrant – working with young children and teenagers who had passed over suddenly, as she had experienced this herself. She was laughing and having a little joke with me.

I was so happy to know Jessica was truly safe and well! It was after this visit to my church that I wrote the second poem.

Gone In An Instant

She's gone in an instant,
no longer in my world.
Her time on earth complete.
Lessons learned
and lessons given.

My heart breaks.
My body aches,
for my baby
my child,
my friend.

My tears dry for a moment.
I lift my head.
A breath away, I see her.
A heartbeat away, I hear her.
She's gone on before me and she lives!

I know that she is whole
and she is beautiful.
I know that she laughs and has fun.
And I know that one day I'll be with her.
But that is not till my time here is done.

And I know that my Jessica would want us,
to live a life that is full.
Make the most of every minute
and like her
be a STAR as a rule.

Composed by Angela January 2011

THE PAIN OF LOSS

I am blessed to have the knowledge that my daughter is safe and well and 'lives' on, but even with this knowledge, I still miss her and think about her constantly. I never realised before losing Jessica that grief can actually produce physical pain.

Although at the time of her 'death' I had the strength to help the family, our friends and Jessica's friends, her loss threatened to overwhelm me about a year later. I was harbouring a desperate feeling of guilt, that, as her mother, I should have been able to keep her safe. I grew weary from not being able to hold her or hear her voice.

My friend the medium helped me to realise that too many tears and prolonged sadness were not helping Jessica to move on. Our laughter and enjoyment of life, enables our deceased loved ones to find peace.

I decided to concentrate on and give thanks for, the twenty two years of Jessica's life spent here on earth, with us.

How lucky we were to have enjoyed many happy holidays together and with our extended family.

Jessica also had the health, imagination and enthusiasm to make the most of all the opportunities that came her way. She worked and travelled while at secondary school and during her time at university. She had a wonderful sense of humour, and a quick wit, which kept her cousins and friends in stitches with laughter.

So I came to write this next poem, which captures the thoughts that have helped me cope from day to day.

The Pain of Loss

Your time had come,
you left this world,
back then it broke my heart.

The pain of loss,
so physical.
Something deep within
was torn apart.

I still see your face
in all I do and
every thought
I share with you.

I guessed in time
I could let you go,
but I'll **always** keep
you near me.

I'll listen each day
to hear what you say
and tell the world
you're not far away
really!

And it fills my soul
with joy to know,
one day,
again,
I'll hug you so!

Composed by Angela - November 2011

STARS GIVING PEOPLE HAPPINESS

Jessica died the day before her twenty second birthday. This date is etched into the memory of all her friends and family. As the anniversary approaches each year, I can feel their concern for us and a tangible tension starts to build. I wanted to do something to help all of us through this difficult time, which holds such unhappy memories.

Usually, around her birthday, everyone would be thinking of sending Jessica a card to celebrate the day. I had the idea to send them a card, with a happy memory of Jessica inside, to arrive on her birthday!

A couple of weeks before this decision, I had been sorting through Jessica's school work. I found a poem she had written when she was eleven and just starting secondary school. I had never read the poem before, but was struck by her reference to STARS bringing people happiness!

I firmly believe she guided me to find the poem, as confirmation of her love, shown through the star signs we have been receiving since she died.

As I write this, I remember that I have actually received a message from Jessica saying how pleased she is that we celebrate her birthday in this way!

I hope you enjoy Jessica's poem Up In Space.

Up In Space

Up in space there is the sun.
A big ball of fire.
Yellow, orange and red.
Melting anything that goes near it.

Up in space there is the moon.
A copper coin on a velvety background.
Bright, shining, fantastic.
Giving people light, at night.

Up in space there are the **stars.**
Little fairy lights splintering the darkness.
Shooting, shining, glistening.
Giving people happiness.

Composed by Jessica – September 2000

A MAGNIFICENT RAINBOW

I would like to conclude this section of the book with a special message from Jessica.

Just after the second anniversary of her death, I felt the need to visit my church.

As I push open the doors, I always feel as if I have come home.
I take my cup of tea and sit quietly in one of the pews, while people chat around me sharing their news.

After the singing of some well known hymns, there may be a reading given by a church member. Following the reading, the medium serving the church that day, will give a short inspirational talk. These shared thoughts are sometimes guided from a higher realm and help me on a day to day basis. They also uplift me spiritually.

A large part of the service is allocated to evidence of 'survival', where the medium will give messages to people attending the church that day, from their deceased loved ones.

On this special day, I was again, very lucky to receive a message from Jessica, confirming she is still close to us and always will be. A few years on and she is now teaching older and younger people parables. This doesn't surprise me, as Jessica studied theology and philosophy in her early teens and ancient history at university. I still keep some of her work, pages of neatly and carefully written handwriting.

As the medium reached the end of his message, he said "She is sending you a rainbow."

I drove home as darkness fell and was filled with love, joy, wonder and hope. A beautiful rainbow filled my thoughts and I knew Jessica was letting me know that one day, I would find her there, at the end of a magnificent rainbow.

SO WHAT HAPPENS NEXT?

SUMMARY

Since time began, man has known instinctively that there must be something more than a black void to look forward to, when we 'die'. What that something is, has remained a mystery.

After all these years of reading, learning and experiencing, I believe 'death' of the physical body is a stage of nature, but not the last stage! When we 'die', the energy, which is the essence of 'us', is released into the next stage!

I find it really exciting to learn that over the last few years, scientists have been searching for the substance which makes up 85% of the known universe, but cannot be seen with the human eye.

This substance is made up of tiny particles of energy, vibrating at different speeds. When we 'die' we move into a different level of vibrations.

A medium seems to be able to tune in to our deceased loved ones, as they lower their vibrations in order to communicate with us. I have learnt that this activity is quite difficult for the deceased to achieve!

As the procedure requires so much effort from both the medium and the deceased, we are truly blessed to receive messages of love and comfort.

Time, as we know it, does not exist in the next stage of 'life'. The deceased have the opportunity to rest when they first pass over and although that may seem a blink of an eye to them, it can be a lifetime for us. Sometimes, no matter how many mediums visited, or signs longed for, contact is never accomplished.

Even though contact is never made, it does not mean that they love us less. One day you will meet again and they will reveal what they have been doing all this time!

After reading this little book, which brings a message of hope, you may decide to visit a medium or attend a Spiritualist church. There are also many Spiritualist centres beginning to open all over the United Kingdom. Many people, who associate a church with religion, may prefer to visit a centre.

Remember, there is good and bad in most areas of life, so it would be helpful to find someone, or a church/centre, that has been recommended to you. Attend with light and love in your heart and if you are in the right place, or with the right medium, you should feel at home.

I hope you have found some comfort and a curiosity to find out more, through reading the poems and hearing about the gift of Jessica's STARS!

I am extremely lucky to know my daughter Jessica is safe, well and continuing her 'life' somewhere out there, in our wonderful, mystical universe…………..

OTHER POEMS

Composed by the Author

I have composed many poems over the years for my family and friends. I like to make them smile and let them know how much they mean to me. The poems are very personal and are greatly enjoyed by them, because of that.

The poems I have chosen to be included in this next section of the book can be enjoyed by everyone! They encourage an appreciation of the present moment and are ultimately, uplifting.

THE KALEIDOSCOPE OF LIFE

Looking through the lens of a kaleidoscope, we see a picture or a pattern made up of amazing shapes and colours. When we twist the lens, the pattern completely changes, instantly.

A few months after Jessica's 'death', the thought came to me that life is like a kaleidoscope.

We go about our everyday routines, taking everything for granted, rushing around, not really seeing or hearing. We never fully appreciate what we have at that moment, until something happens that changes the pattern of our lives.

The 'death' of a close family member or friend can seriously alter the balance of relationships within a whole family. Everyone touched by the loss is changed in some way and a new pattern emerges.

Happy, positive events such as the birth of a child, marriage, new jobs, new friends, also bring change into our lives and therefore, the lives of those close to us.

Enjoying coffee with a friend one day, I started to describe my thoughts on this idea, when she suggested I write a poem about it.

I hope you enjoy The Kaleidoscope of Life.

Kaleidoscope of Life

As we look at our lives
and we strive to cope,
it feels just like
a kaleidoscope.

One moment things seem
to be going so well,
then something will change
and we're going through hell.

Patterns and colours
dance through our lives,
changing and twisting
through our laughs and
our cries.

Sometimes the colours
may seem too bright.
We have to change,
re-adjust,
till things turn out right.

As we stop at each turn,
see the beauty within it.
Take a breath,
embrace it now,
it may be gone in a minute.

Composed by Angela July 2011

THE BIKE RIDE

When our children were very young, we started to visit the Peak District as a family. Once a year, we rented a small cottage nestled amongst the little tea shops and streams of a pretty village, surrounded by hills and craggy mountains

Every day, if the weather permitted, we would take a picnic and walk or cycle over those hills. The children had such little legs and walked in their wellington boots, so in those early years a relatively short walk could take hours!

I was concerned when my husband suggested we take them on a trek to the top of Kinder Scout, one of the highest Peaks in the area. This took us on a long winding path through a valley beside a gushing stream full of huge boulders. When the stream reached the mountainside, we faced a perilously steep climb, over slippery slate, to reach the summit! Our son thoroughly enjoyed these scrambles, but Jessica always needed lots of encouragement and a promise of chocolate or an ice cream at the end of the journey!

A favourite outing for us was a bike ride around a large reservoir. The circular ride covers twelve miles and hugs the edge of the reservoir, which is home to a spectacular dam. Surrounded by hills and trees that glow in the autumn sunshine, the ride, with the children, took us about three hours to complete.

I have to say that Jessica found this outing a bit of a nightmare! We had to coax her along with lots of cuddles, but there were many tears shed along those hilly paths!

Later on, when Jessica was a teenager, she completed her Bronze Duke of Edinburgh Award. This entailed trekking over the Peaks with a group of school friends and sleeping in a tent for two or three nights. We were very proud of her and wondered at the time, who supplied all the ice cream!

The poem The Bike Ride paints a picture of the journey around the reservoir, past the spot where we used to sit by the stream on a fallen tree trunk and share our picnic with the many ducks waddling about on the grassy banks.

Sheep would be grazing all over the hillside along the path. During the spring, we would see many tiny lambs, staying close to their mothers, as we pedalled by as a family.

On this particular ride, the children were in their early teens. It started to rain quite heavily and we decided to forge ahead and make it to the comfort of the car and the short drive home to a warm bath.

At the end of the ride, I was exhilarated and felt great to be at one with nature. Whereas the rest of my party, were wet and cold and very ready to go home!

This particular cycle ride was a good example of how people can participate in exactly the same experience, but feel so differently about it. Jessica refused to come on this ride thereafter!

Enjoy the Bike Ride.

The Bike Ride

The cascading wall of white
that is the dam, greets us,
as we push our bikes up through the trees
to the path,
we're off!
To our left, the dark waters of the reservoir.
To our right and as far as the eye can see,
a vista of the reds, golds and rusts of the autumn
leaves.

The path hugs the lakeside,
stony and hard.
Clusters of vagabond sheep scatter before us,
curious, but unafraid.
We reach the bridge.
The stream plays over the rocks,
but no stopping today,
it looks like rain!

The second half of the journey,
we pass the ducks, eager for our lunch!
The road, easier now, smooth and winding.
Down comes the rain!
On go our waterproofs!
Pedalling harder!
We WHIZ down the slopes,
rain in our eyes,
wind on our faces.

I AM THE WIND!
I AM THE RAIN!
You are all cold and wet!
We love the ride.
We love each other.

(Clearly, this was only my opinion!)

Composed by Angela - January 2008

HOW IT IS FOR ME

One afternoon a few years ago, I was sitting alone in our garden in the sunshine, when I decided to write this poem about how I feel sometimes.

I am a worrier and at times, become very anxious over imagined outcomes. I know this worrying uses needless energy and I have to work at maintaining a healthy outlook on life.

Our generation lives in a fast moving environment, on constant call from telephone, texts, e mails and news from television, radio and the papers. Sometimes I feel that I can't process any more information and begin to struggle. I have to make a conscious effort to calm things down, get the balance back into my everyday life and just take one day at a time.

I am never happier than when we visit our rented cottage in the Peaks, surrounded by nature and a slower pace of life. We only visit this little cottage once or twice a year, but it is a haven of peace and tranquillity.

Although Jessica disliked the walking and cycling through the countryside, she did enjoy the peace and quiet of the cottage. In the evenings, the four of us would walk through the village to a nearby pub, sit by the fire and share a meal. We would talk about the scramble up the mountainside, the slippery crossing of a stream. Later in the evening, we would head back to the cottage feeling warm and content from the meal and play cards at the kitchen table.

The next poem expresses how important it is to have quiet time in your life to enjoy the simple pleasures of nature.

How It Is For Me

My mind is full of the clutter and chatter
of everyday life.
Worries greet me with the sun
and torment me through the day.

Decisions await me at every turn.
Events loom before me like hurdles in a race.
My soul is clouded by my thoughts.
I cannot live.

There is a place.
A valley of green and rusty hills.
A small house says welcome,
stay and rest.

I HEAR the larks, the church bells,
the gurgle of the stream and the bleating of the lambs,
as they gambol in the farmer's field.

I SEE lazy ducks amongst the willow,
heads tucked under their wings.
Gliders high in the sky, circling in the summer
breeze.

I FEEL the rain on my face,
my aching limbs, as I come down from the
mountainside.
The sun wakes me gently,
and I LIVE.

Composed by Angela July 2007

FOREVER TWENTY ONE

Christmas can be a very difficult time for families who have been bereaved. Expectations are for everybody to gather together, family and friends, to share love, presents and laughter. The fact that your loved one will never share this special time with you again, can produce an overwhelming sadness at this time of year. Although I still enjoy Christmas, I am very glad when this season comes to an end.

One day in January, I watched through the window, as the rain and wind brought havoc to the garden. Thinking of Jessica, the thought came into my mind that she would be twenty one forever, as she had died the day before her twenty second birthday.

This thought conjured up a picture of Jessica frozen in time and then I quickly realised, this was not the reality Jessica had come back to reveal to us.

Even as a child, I rationalised that the essence of 'us' with all the energy that it takes to live, surely could not be extinguished when we die. As I look back at all the love, laughter, tears and other emotions I shared with Jessica during her life time here with us, I now know this as a truth.

I began to write the poem Forever Twenty One.

Forever Twenty One

Days turn into years
and she is frozen in time.
Forever twenty one
in the depths of my mind.

But, no, I can see her
as she runs
and she plays.
Giggles with her friends
in those early days.

Learning to swim,
then riding a bike.
Walking the hills,
though she hated to hike!

The banging of doors,
the stamping of feet.
The rows as a teenager
now remembered so sweet.

A home of her own,
where she cooked
and she cleaned!
A stir in her heart
of love, no longer
a dream.

45

All this 'life' can't be frozen,
she will continue to shine,
out there in the cosmos,
her journey divine.

Composed by Angela – January 2014

CONCLUSION

The direction of my life has gravitated towards a spiritual path of investigation into what happens to us when we 'die'.

With the greatest joy, I must conclude, through my own experiences and Jessica's continued communication from another 'level of energy', that the course of nature requires us to continue our existence after the 'death' of the physical body.

I firmly believe though, that our time here on earth is precious and we should live it to the very best of our ability. Kindness, understanding and generosity to our family, friends, and neighbours should be our most important endeavour. If this undertaking could be achieved, love and goodness would ripple out across the planet and one day, the world really could be a better place.

******

Writing the poems and lacing them together throughout the true story revealing Jessica's continued existence, has helped me cope with her loss.

The unconditional love that Jessica and I share and the loving intentions of the mediums, have built a bridge of love between two worlds.

With love from Angela – Jessica's mum x

Photograph on Front Cover: Jessica

Lightning Source UK Ltd.
Milton Keynes UK
UKOW04f1733290118
317020UK00001B/14/P

9 781785 073816